Workbook for the RESTORATION IDEAL

by Marshall Leggett

Author of

Introduction to the RESTORATION IDEAL

Edited by Timothy A. Heck

Illustrated by Dan Dunham

From The Library of Greg Cheatham

STANDARD PUBLISHING
Cincinnati, Ohio   3176

Sharing the thoughts of his own heart, the author may express views not entirely consistent with those of the publisher.

ISBN 0-87403-068-4

Copyright © 1986. The STANDARD PUBLISHING Company, Cincinnati, Ohio. A division of STANDEX INTERNATIONAL Corporation. Printed in U.S.A.

TABLE OF CONTENTS

Preface.. 5

Introduction to the Restoration Ideal...................... 7

The Church for Which Christ Gave Himself.................. 11

Barton Warren Stone and the Ancient Name.................. 15

The Name "Christian"...................................... 19

Thomas Campbell: Man of the Book.......................... 23

The Bible: God's Word and Man's Guide..................... 27

Alexander Campbell and the Ancient Order.................. 31

The Ancient Order of Things............................... 35

Walter Scott and the Ancient Gospel....................... 39

Sin... 43

Grace... 47

Faith... 51

Repentance.. 55

The Good Confession....................................... 59

The Meaning of Christian Baptism.......................... 63

The Mode and Subjects of Christian Baptism................ 67

The Holy Spirit... 71

Membership and Ministry................................... 75

Evangelism and Discipleship............................... 79

Christian Worship... 83

Church Government... 87

Christian Stewardship..................................... 91

The Acappella Churches of Christ.......................... 95

The Disciples of Christ................................... 99

The Charismatics.. 103

The Fantastic Future for the Restoration Ideal............ 107

PREFACE

This Workbook is designed to be used with Dr. Marshall Leggett's textbook, *Introduction to the Restoration Ideal*. We recommend studying through the book and workbook one chapter at a time. Here are a few ways in which the study may be done:

Sunday-school Class

Introduction to the Restoration Ideal provides a thorough curriculum for use in an adult elective class over two quarters (twenty-six weeks).

Home Bible Study

Plan to incorporate the study into your home Bible-study group. The questions in the workbook will stimulate excellent discussion.

Leadership Training

Many church leaders have never undertaken a study of the restoration movement. This series enables elders, deacons, teachers, and others in leadership positions to gain insight into the restoration ideal.

Personal Study

Use the text and the workbook in your personal study time to enhance your own understanding of restoration principles. Perhaps you could invite a friend to join you once a week and share your newfound knowledge with each other.

Each chapter in the workbook is composed of six sections. The following explanation of each section will help you get the most out of your study through each:

What to Expect

This section gives suggested objectives for the chapter.

Key Verses

These Scripture passages express the Biblical principles on which the chapter is built. It is recommended that you **memorize** these verses.

Recapitulation

This statement helps to summarize the previous chapter and relate it to the present one.

Dealing With the Issues

This is the main section of the chapter, designed to stimulate research and thought through a variety of questions and exercises. Take some time on this section, and be sure you understand the facts it highlights.

Your Turn for Questions

Each chapter allows space for you to write some questions of your own about what you have studied in the text. Share your questions with your teacher, group leader, or study partner. If you are studying on your own, ask your minister or some other leader your questions.

What About You?

This section challenges you to make personal application of the content of each chapter. You could get into some very beneficial discussions as you wrestle with these questions. If you're not in a class, be sure to find someone with whom you can discuss these concepts.

Introducing—John Q. Disciple

John Q. Disciple will lead you through each lesson as he also discovers the restoration ideal.

We think you'll find *Introduction to the Restoration Ideal* and *Workbook for the Restoration Ideal* a fascinating learning experience that will increase your appreciation for New Testament Christianity.

—The Editor

Chapter One

INTRODUCTION TO THE RESTORATION IDEAL

The Restoration Ideal leads John Q. Disciple to a Biblical, undenominational faith.

Key Verses

"Neither pray I for these alone, but for them also which shall believe on me through their word; that they all may be one; as thou, Father, art in me, and I in thee, that they also may be one in us: that the world may believe that thou hast sent me."

John 17:20, 21

What to Expect

An understanding of what is meant by the word *ideal* in reference to the church.

An appreciation for the unity of the first-century church.

Dealing With the Issues

A. Consider the statement from chapter 1 of the text (**Introduction to the Restoration Ideal,** #3175) regarding the restoration movement: "It may well have the greatest plea on earth, but it could be that its people are the stingiest with it."

1. Do you agree with this appraisal? Explain.

   _____

   _____

   _____

2. If you agree with the statement, how have you seen it evidenced in the church today?

   _____

   _____

B. Notice the text's discussion of ideals and restoration.

1. How would you define the word *ideal*?

   _____

   _____

2. What is our model for restoring the church?

   _____

   _____

3. What is the significance of the term *restoration*? How does it compare with *reformation*?

   _____

   _____

   _____

4. Do you believe it is possible to restore fully the New Testament church? Explain.

   _____

   _____

   _____

5. What can be learned from the following illustration of the antique chair?

   Restoration means bringing back to the original condition. It recognizes that the present state is not what it ought to be. For example, a piece of furniture, perhaps a chair, may be found in the attic. It has been abused as it was passed down the family from generation to generation. Its finish is marred, and some of its joints may have loosened. It doesn't look like much, and it fails in its purpose. No one can sit in it because of its weakened condition. Then, continuing our illustration, a connoisseur of antique furniture spots it. He sees in his mind's eye what the chair could be if it were restored to its original state.

   He takes it to his workshop and begins to work on it. It is hard because the chair is in bad repair, but he labors patiently, correcting his own mistakes as he makes them. He does not try to change the chair's original form, or alter what it was in the beginning. Instead, he keeps working toward that ideal as he envisions it to have been at its inception. When he finishes, he does not have merely a reproduction, a copy of the original. Instead, he has something much better—the restoration of that which the original builder intended (page 11).

   How does this illustration relate to the mission of the church?

   _____

   _____

   _____

6. What are a few of the obstacles that have prevented the church from fulfilling the restoration ideal?

   _____

   _____

C. Jesus said, "I will build My church" (Matthew 16:18).

1. What are the implications of such a grand statement?

   _____

   _____

   _____

2. What role does Jesus Christ fulfill in the church?

3. How does man tend to usurp the ecclesiastical authority of Christ?

4. What safeguards should be incorporated into church practice to deter such a blasphemous possibility?

5. How can the church accomplish the unity for which Jesus prayed in John 17?

6. What indication do we have that even the apostles struggled with division in their ministries?

7. What are some of the issues that result in division in the church today?

8. What is the ultimate goal of Christian unity?

D. List some principles we can adopt from the way in which the apostles dealt with the potentially explosive issue in Acts 6.

1.

2.

3.

4.

Your Turn for Questions

What questions do you have about what you have studied in chapter 1?

What About You?

1. What can you do to increase your understanding of New Testament Christianity?

   _____

   _____

   _____

2. What can you do to bring greater unity in your own local congregation?

   _____

   _____

   _____

CHRISTIANS MUST BECOME ONE IN ORDER FOR THE WORLD TO BE WON!

Chapter Two

THE CHURCH FOR WHICH CHRIST GAVE HIMSELF

Key Verses

"Husbands, love your wives, even as Christ also loved the church, and gave himself for it; that he might sanctify and cleanse it with the washing of water by the word, that he might present it to himself a glorious church, not having spot, or wrinkle, or any such thing; but that it should be holy and without blemish."

Ephesians 5:25-27

Recapitulation: The restoration ideal leads to the essential marks of the New Testament church.

What to Expect

A review of the church's beginnings.

An overview of church history and its digression from first-century ideals.

A look at Martin Luther's bold attempt for reformation of the church, as well as other more recent attempts for unity.

Dealing With the Issues

A. It is not possible to separate Christianity from the church of Jesus Christ, though many have tried to do just that in practice and in doctrine.

1. What happens to an individual at the point of conversion?
   a. He is saved.

   b. _____

   c. _____

   d. _____

   e. _____

2. How can we best understand Christ's meaning in the words, "Upon this rock I will build my church?"

   _____

   _____

   _____

3. What statements are there in Scripture that reveal Christ's love for the church?

   _____

   _____

   _____

4. The Day of Pentecost, A.D. 30, marked the occasion of several events. What are some of the activities that transpired on that historic day?

   _____

   _____

   _____

5. According to Acts 6:7, what two consequences resulted from the influence of apostolic leadership?

   a. _____

   _____

   b. _____

B. Corruption does not always result from external influences alone. Often it is a cancer from within that poses the greatest threat.

1. What have you learned in this chapter about Emperor Constantine?

   _____

   _____

   _____

   _____

2. What did the "Edict of Toleration" do in A.D. 313?

   _____

   _____

   _____

3. The secularization of Christianity continues to the present. To what signs can you point that would reveal such a blending?

   _____

   _____

   _____

4. Comment briefly about the following:

   a. The Council of Nicea _____
   _____

   b. Leo I _____
   _____

   c. Bishop of Constantinople _____
   _____

   d. Leo III _____
   _____

C. A glance at church history shows that God has always raised up spokesmen to challenge His people with Biblical purity.

1. To what did Martin Luther react so vehemently that motivated him to face even excommunication from the Roman Catholic church? Explain.

   _____
   _____
   _____
   _____

2. List the three emphases of Luther's Protestant Reformation and give your own interpretation of each.

   a. _____
   _____
   _____

   b. _____
   _____
   _____

   c. _____
   _____
   _____

3. What would you cite as some of the major reasons that the efforts of the ecumenical movement failed?

   _____
   _____
   _____
   _____
   _____
   _____

4. What were some of the positive results of the ecumenical movement?

   _____
   _____
   _____
   _____
   _____
   _____
   _____

5. What difference do you detect between the former restorative attempts and the restoration movement? (Note the text's brief introduction given at the close of chapter 2.)

   _____
   _____
   _____
   _____
   _____
   _____

Your Turn for Questions

What questions do you have about what you have studied in chapter two?

_____
_____
_____
_____

What About You?

How has your Christianity become "secularized," or blended with the world?

_____
_____
_____
_____

**JESUS LOVES THE CHURCH
HE GAVE THE APOSTLES TO OVERSEE**

Chapter Three

BARTON WARREN STONE AND THE ANCIENT NAME

John Q. Disciple meets Barton W. Stone

Key Verses

"And the Gentiles shall see thy righteousness, and all kings thy glory: and thou shalt be called by a new name, which the mouth of the Lord shall name.

"Even unto them will I give in mine house and within my walls a place and a name better than of sons and of daughters: I will give them an everlasting name, that shall not be cut off."

Isaiah 62:2 and 56:5

Recapitulation: Jesus loves the church He gave the apostles to oversee.

What to Expect

An introduction to Barton W. Stone as a leader in the nineteenth-century restoration movement.

A brief summary of a few of the anti-Biblical doctrines of the church in the early nineteenth century.

Dealing With the Issues

A. Helpful to understanding the early restorers is a knowledge of their personal pasts, especially with respect to the church.

1. Give some of the family background of Barton W. Stone.

   _____

   _____

2. What was the key difference between McGready's preaching and that of William Hodge? Why did Hodge's preaching have more effect on Stone?

   _____

   _____

3. How did Stone respond when he was asked whether he would "receive and adopt the Westminster Confession of Faith"?

   _____

   _____

4. What is your opinion of his response?

   _____

   _____

B. Nineteenth-century revivalism.

1. What was the reason for the rise of the camp meetings?

   _____

   _____

2. Describe some of the happenings at the Cane Ridge Revival.

   _____

   _____

   _____

3. How did Stone's evangelistic appeal differ from that of the orthodox Presbyterians?

   _____

   _____

   _____

4. The Presbyterian Synod brought charges against two revival men. Who were they, and what was the thrust of their protest against the Synod?

   _____

   _____

   _____

   _____

5. Upon leaving the Synod, what was their first action?

   _____

   _____

   _____

C. Restoration beginnings.

1. How many congregations made up the Springfield Presbytery, and how long did it remain in existence?

   _____

   _____

2. What is the name of the document written in connection with the Presbytery's dissolution?

3. List the three items from the document mentioned in the text (page 30), and give your own interpretation of each.

    a. _____

    b. _____

    c. _____

4. What would you consider Barton Stone's greatest contribution to the movement?

5. What journal did Barton Stone publish?

6. What is the significance of what took place over the New Year's holiday of 1832 in the Christian Church on Hill Street in Lexington, Kentucky?

7. How did Alexander Campbell appraise the meeting of 1832?

8. What did A. G. Comings write of Barton Stone at his death?

Your Turn for Questions

What questions do you have about what you have studied in chapter three?

What About You?

1. What were some of your earliest impressions of Christianity? How have they changed?

2. How does the church continue to be affected by the creeds of man?

_____

_____

_____

3. What does it mean to you to be a "Christian" only?

_____

_____

_____

BARTON W. STONE SAW A VISION OF ALL BELIEVERS UNITED AS "CHRISTIANS" ONLY

Chapter Four
THE NAME "CHRISTIAN"

A Christian only! What else is there?

Key Verse

"If a man suffer as a Christian, let him not be ashamed, but let him glorify God in this name."

1 Peter 4:16, ASV

Recapitulation: Barton W. Stone said persons can be Christians only.

What to Expect

An appreciation of how a person's name distinguishes him as an individual.

A realization that "Christian" is the divinely-appointed name for Jesus' followers.

Dealing With the Issues

A. "One's name distinguishes him from others; it contains all that he is and represents the sum total of his personality."

1. Do you agree with the above statement taken from our text (page 35)? Explain.

   _____

   _____

   _____

2. If you were to rename yourself, what name would you choose and why?

   _____

   _____

   _____

3. List some names used in Scripture for God.

   _____

   _____

   _____

   _____

4. Do you recall the meaning of these names?

   a. Hoshea:_____

   b. Joshua:_____

   c. Abram:_____

   d. Abraham:_____

   e. Jacob:_____

   f. Israel:_____

   g. Simon:_____

   h. Peter:_____

   i. Saul:_____

   j. Paul:_____

5. What was the Hebrew name for Jesus, and what does it mean?

   _____

   _____

   _____

B. Because of what has been established about names, it was a critical decision what the followers of Jesus were to be called. The name is a divinely-appointed one, signifying our relationship to Christ himself.

1. What is the message in each of the following verses?

   a. Isaiah 65:15:_____

   _____

   b. Isaiah 62:2:_____

   _____

   c. Isaiah 56:5:_____

   _____

   d. Amos 9:12:_____

   _____

   e. Acts 15:16-18:_____

   _____

2. What were some of the various names by which the followers of Jesus were called?

   _____

   _____

   _____

   _____

3. Why were none of these names the fulfillment of the prophecies?

   _____

   _____

   _____

4. How does our text interpret the words of Acts 11:26, and what is the significance of the Greek term *chrematizo*?

_____

_____

_____

5. What did Barton W. Stone think about the name "Christian"?

_____

_____

6. Thomas Campbell favored the use of the name "Christian" for two reasons. What were they?

a. _____

_____

b. _____

_____

7. What additional testimony do we have from church history to verify the name "Christian" as the divinely-given name for Jesus' followers?

_____

_____

_____

8. The text states that the name "Christian" is both inclusive and exclusive.

a. How is it inclusive? _____

_____

b. How is it exclusive? _____

_____

Your Turn for Questions

What questions do you have about what you have studied in chapter four?

_____

_____

_____

_____

What About You?

1. Today, those who would follow Jesus are called by numerous different names and labels. Why do you think these variants arose?

_____

_____

_____

2. We can profane the name of the Lord by what we say; but as people who bear the name of the Lord, we can also profane His name through what we do. In what ways do Christians sometimes profane God?

_____

_____

_____

3. How can you better fulfill Peter's admonition to "glorify God in this name" (1 Peter 4:16, ASV)?

_____

_____

_____

PERSONS CAN BE "CHRISTIANS" ONLY

Chapter Five

THOMAS CAMPBELL, MAN OF THE BOOK

John Q. Disciple meets Thomas Campbell

Key Verses

"All Scripture is given by inspiration of God, and is profitable for doctrine, for reproof, for correction, for instruction in righteousness: that the man of God may be perfect, thoroughly furnished unto all good works."
2 Timothy 3:16, 17

Recapitulation: Persons can be "Christians" only.

What to Expect

A brief review of Thomas Campbell's life as it relates to his involvement in the restoration movement.

An overview of the *Declaration and Address* as a vital document in the initial stages of the movement.

Dealing With the Issues

A. Thomas Campbell has been characterized as the creator of the restoration movement. His wisdom is demonstrated in his marvelous statement, "Where the Scriptures speak, we speak; where the Scriptures are silent, we are silent."

1. What does this slogan mean to you personally?

   _____

   _____

2. Why is this statement so critical in the restoration movement?

   _____

   _____

3. Describe Thomas Campbell's religious upbringing?

   _____

   _____

   _____

   _____

4. Comment on Thomas Campbell's experience recorded by Robert Richardson.
   He was one day walking alone in the fields, when, in the midst of his prayerful anxieties and longings, he felt a divine peace suddenly diffuse itself throughout his soul, and the love of God seemed to be shed abroad in his heart as he had never realized it. His doubts, anxieties and fears were at once dissipated, and as if by enchantment. He was enabled to see and to trust in the merits of a crucified Christ, and to enjoy a divine sense of reconciliation, that filled him with rapture, and seemed to determine his destiny for ever. From this moment he recognized himself as consecrated to God, and thought only how he might best appropriate his time and his abilities to his service.[1]

   _____

   _____

[1]Robert Richardson, *Memoirs of Alexander Campbell* (Cincinnati: Standard Publishing, 1868), Vol. I, p. 22.

5. Given Campbell's educational and vocational background, what kind of a minister do you think he was? Describe him as you picture him in your own mind.

   _____

   _____

   _____

   _____

B. When you resolve to take a stand for what you believe to be right, you will inevitably encounter opposition. Thomas Campbell represents a model witnessing to the truth of that statement.

1. Do you agree with his appraisal of church division, that it is "an evil of no small magnitude . . . hurtful . . . and . . . embarrassing?" Explain.

   _____

   _____

   _____

   _____

2. Describe the events that led to Campbell's censorship from the Chartiers Presbytery, and give your own opinion of his actions.

   _____

   _____

   _____

   _____

   _____

3. If you had been Thomas Campbell on September 14, 1808, how might you have felt given his circumstances?

   _____

   _____

   _____

4. In light of the extreme denominationalism and extensive practice of creeds, how do you think that small audience responded to Campbell's exhortation at the home of Abraham Altars in Washington, Pennsylvania?

_____

_____

_____

_____

C. The Declaration and Address comprises one of the most extensive documents of the movement and one of the most descriptive. Use the thirteen points listed in the text as a basis for you to write your own understanding or paraphrase of each below.

1. _____

_____

2. _____

_____

3. _____

_____

4. _____

_____

5. _____

_____

6. _____

_____

7. _____

_____

8. _____

_____

9. _____

_____

10. _____

_____

11. _____

_____

12. _____

_____

13. _____

_____

Your Turn for Questions

What questions do you have about what you have studied in chapter five?

_____

_____

_____

_____

_____

_____

_____

_____

_____

_____

_____

_____

_____

_____

_____

What About You?

1. Looking around your own set of circumstances, what wrong confronts you in society, or perhaps even the church? What will you do about correcting that wrong?

   _____

   _____

   _____

2. If you could write a statement that would be read by everyone caught up in denominationalism, what would you say?

   _____

   _____

   _____

**THOMAS CAMPBELL BELIEVED
PERSONS COULD BE "CHRISTIANS" ONLY
IF THEY WOULD BUT FOLLOW THE BIBLE ONLY**

Chapter Six

THE BIBLE: GOD'S WORD AND MAN'S GUIDE

Key Verses

"How then shall they call on him in whom they have not believed? And how shall they believe in him of whom they have not heard? And how shall they hear without a preacher? . . . So then faith cometh by hearing, and hearing by the word of God."

Romans 10:14, 17

Recapitulation: Persons can be "Christians" only if they will but follow the Bible only.

What to Expect

A presentation of the Bible as the authoritative and inspired Word of God.

The challenge to respond obediently to the message of the Scriptures.

Dealing With the Issues

A. Scripture is a unique book in that it finds its source in the very person of God. Like no other piece of literature, it reveals truths that would be otherwise unknown were it not for its existence.

1. What is meant by the Greek word *musterion?*

   _____
   _____
   _____

2. What is the meaning of the term *revelation?*

   _____
   _____
   _____

3. Why did God choose this particular medium of communication to reveal His will?

   _____
   _____
   _____

B. The New Testament writers confirm the fact of creation as a result of the spoken word of God. The Hebrews writer also affirms that the world itself is upheld by "the word of his power" (Hebrews 1:3).

How does each of the following passages relate to this concept?

1. John 1:1, 3: _____
   _____

2. John 1:10: _____
   _____

3. Genesis 1:1: _____
   _____

4. Genesis 1:3, 9: _____
   _____

5. Jeremiah 23:29: _____
   _____

6. John 1:14: _____
   _____

7. John 14:8-10: _____
   _____

8. Colossians 2:9: _____
   _____

9. Hebrews 1:3: _____
   _____

C. The early prophets had the privilege of direct communication with the Lord. The disciples of Jesus were able to converse personally with the Lord Jesus Christ.

1. How has God met this need for communication since the ascension of our Lord?

   _____
   _____
   _____

2. Explain the meaning of *inspiration*.

   _____
   _____
   _____
   _____

3. What is the purpose of the Bible, written Word of God?

   _____
   _____
   _____

4. What was the main objective of the Old Testament?

_____
_____
_____

D. The Scripture is the inspired, authoritative Word of God. It is His only revelation of himself, His will, and His love for man, and is completely reliable.

1. Second Peter 1:21 provides the answer for how this reliability could be possible. What is the key to the Bible's truthfulness?

_____
_____
_____

2. What did the discovery of the Dead Sea Scrolls do to verify the authenticity of Scripture?

_____
_____
_____

E. The Scriptures are invaluable in the Christian's life as the guide to true maturity in Christ. What do the following passages reveal to us about the Bible?

1. 2 Timothy 2:15_____
_____

2. 2 Timothy 3:15_____
_____

3. 2 Timothy 3:16_____
_____

4. 2 Timothy 3:17_____
_____

5. 2 Timothy 4:2_____
_____

Your Turn for Questions

What questions do you have about what you have studied in chapter six?

_____
_____
_____
_____
_____

What About You?

1. How does it make you feel about yourself to know that the infinite and eternal God has communicated to you and made His will known to you through His Word?

_____
_____

2. How well have you done in your personal devotion to study and application of God's revealed will in the Scriptures? Will you write out your pledge to God, telling Him what you intend to do from here on out regarding His Word to you?

_____
_____

THE BIBLE IS THE ONLY RULE OF FAITH AND PRACTICE FOR CHRISTIANS

Chapter Seven

ALEXANDER CAMPBELL AND THE ANCIENT ORDER

John Q. Disciple meets Alexander Campbell

Key Verse

"And Jesus answered and said unto him, Blessed art thou, Simon Bar-jona: for flesh and blood hath not revealed it unto thee, but my Father which is in heaven. And I say also unto thee, That thou art Peter, and upon this rock I will build my church; and the gates of hell shall not prevail against it."
Matthew 16:17, 18

Recapitulation: Persons can be Christians only if they will but follow the Bible only.

What to Expect

A brief summary of the life of Alexander Campbell as it relates to his involvement in the restoration movement.

An appreciation of the place of Scripture in the life and practice of the Christian.

Dealing With the Issues

A. Alexander Campbell was a unique breed about whom many great words have and still could be said. His early years were filled with mixed influences and circumstances that served, in later years, to be an apt preparation for his work in the ministry.

1. What have you learned about the boyhood of Alexander Campbell?

   _____
   _____
   _____
   _____
   _____

2. What influence did Robert and James Haldane have upon Campbell?

   _____
   _____
   _____
   _____

3. What do you imagine was going through both Thomas' and Alexander's minds as they anticipated their meeting in America?

   _____
   _____
   _____
   _____
   _____

B. It is unfortunate that our natural inclination is to neglect the study of the Scriptures until we are faced head on, as it were, with a time of crisis or need. Such was the case with Alexander Campbell, when his first child was born and he was faced with the question of infant baptism.

1. What were his findings regarding infant baptism?

   _____
   _____
   _____

2. What was Thomas Campbell's attitude and response to the issue of baptism?

   _____
   _____
   _____

C. The publication of pamphlets and books became an important facet of the restoration movement. (We will see more of this dimension in future studies.)

1. What was the purpose of the series, "The Restoration of the Ancient Order of Things?"

   _____
   _____
   _____

2. What was the philosophy of Bethany College?

   _____
   _____
   _____

3. What was the result of Campbell's involvement in the debates?

   _____
   _____
   _____

4. Based on the testimonies of his friends, relatives, and associates, what do you think was the overall purpose for which Alexander Campbell strived in life?

_____

_____

_____

_____

_____

D. So much can be gained through an increased knowledge of the great men of the faith. Do some personal research into the life of Alexander Campbell and find out some more facts about his life and ministry. Record them below.

_____

_____

_____

_____

_____

_____

_____

_____

Your Turn for Questions

What questions do you have about what you have studied in chapter seven?

_____

_____

_____

_____

_____

What About You?

1. Alexander Campbell spent hours devoted to the memorization of large portions of Scripture. How much of the Scripture can you quote from memory? Choose one verse each day this week and begin the profitable practice of hiding God's Word in your heart.

2. Are you facing a time of crisis in your life, or a time of need? Lay that need before the Lord and spend time in His Word this week to find His answers and direction for you.

   Crisis or Need:_____

   Answers:_____

   _____

   _____

3. Take your last name and use it to make an acrostic, as was done for Campbell. Let the acrostic represent your life for Christ as you desire it to be. Pray for His strength to complement your willingness.

**PERSONS CAN BE CHRISTIANS ONLY
IF THEY WILL BUT FOLLOW THE BIBLE ONLY, DO BIBLE THINGS
IN BIBLE WAYS, AND CALL BIBLE THINGS BY BIBLE NAMES**

Chapter Eight

THE ANCIENT ORDER OF THINGS

Let's go back to the church as it was given.

Key Verses

"And I say also unto thee, That thou art Peter, and upon this rock I will build my church; and the gates of hell shall not prevail against it."
                                                                                    Matthew 16:18

"Now I beseech you, brethren, by the name of our Lord Jesus Christ, that ye all speak the same thing, and that there be no divisions among you; but that ye be perfectly joined together in the same mind and in the same judgment."
                                                                                    1 Corinthians 1:10

Recapitulation: Persons can be Christians only if they will but follow the Bible only and do Bible things in Bible ways and call Bible things by Bible names.

What to Expect

An understanding of the distinction between Campbell's attempts for restoration and Luther's attempts for reformation.

A realization of denominationalism as a deterrent to the unity for which our Lord prayed.

Dealing With the Issues

A. Campbell had a burning desire to see Christians united in Jesus Christ around the authority of the Word.

1. What two facts did Campbell note in the high priestly prayer of Jesus (John 17)?

   a. _____

   _____

   _____

   b. _____

   _____

   _____

2. What is the message in 1 Corinthians 1:10?

   _____

   _____

   _____

3. What was the vision that Barton W. Stone sought to attain?

   _____

   _____

   _____

4. What was Thomas Campbell's earnest desire for Christians?

   _____

   _____

   _____

5. How did Alexander Campbell build upon the twin foundations of his father and Stone?

   _____

   _____

   _____

B. Alexander Campbell had great admiration for the earlier reformers of Christianity, yet he also found fault with their approach.

1. What was the method of reformation of men like Luther and Zwingli?

   _____

   _____

   _____

2. Cite, by example, how Luther carried out this practice.

   _____

   _____

   _____

3. What was Campbell's main objection to Martin Luther's attempt at reformation?

   _____

   _____

4. What was the method of approach to restoration that Campbell proposed?

   _____

   _____

5. Where did Campbell believe the ideal church could be found?

_____

_____

C. Campbell not only proposed a restoration of the ancient order of the church, rather he set out to accomplish his goal.

1. What was the two-fold emphasis of the series, "The Restoration of the Ancient Order of Things?"

   a. _____

   _____

   b. _____

   _____

2. What were the two tests to determine the legitimacy of any article of faith or action within the church?

   a. _____

   b. _____

3. Give an example of each of these tests.

   _____

   _____

   _____

4. Campbell pursued the goal of a movement. What was the one possibility in his work which he abhorred?

   _____

   _____

Your Turn for Questions

What questions do you have about what you have studied in chapter eight?

_____

_____

_____

_____

_____

_____

What About You?

1. Christian unity begins on our own front step. Consider those in your own sphere of relationships with whom you are divided for one reason or another. Determine through a written promise to go and make peace with that brother or sister.

   _____

   _____

   _____

2. If we are to take Campbell seriously, we must be willing to abandon all human institutions in our attempt to restore Christ's church. In your own ministry—whether you have a vocational ministry or serve in the "priesthood of all beluevers"—take the time to restudy, rethink, and reapply the commands and precedents found in the New Testament church. What are you going to have to change?

   _____

   _____

   _____

**CHRISTIAN UNITY DEPENDS UPON THE RESTORATION
OF THE ESSENTIAL MARKS OF THE NEW TESTAMENT CHURCH
AS THEY WERE GIVEN TO THE APOSTLES**

Chapter Nine

WALTER SCOTT AND THE ANCIENT GOSPEL

Key Verse

"For I am not ashamed of the gospel of Christ: for it is the power of God unto salvation to every one that believeth; to the Jew first, and also to the Greek."

Romans 1:16

Recapitulation: Christians must seek to do Bible things in Bible ways and call Bible things by Bible names.

What to Expect

A heightened respect for Walter Scott as the restorer of the ancient gospel.

A renewed zeal for the proclamation of the gospel of Jesus Christ.

Dealing With the Issues

A. The restorative work of Barton W. Stone, Thomas Campbell, and Alexander Campbell had done much to advance the cause of the movement, yet Walter Scott was destined to add another crucial dimension to the foundation they had laid.

1. What is Walter Scott noted for restoring, and what title was given to him?

   _____
   _____
   _____

2. Describe Scott's first confrontation with Biblical restoration.

   _____
   _____
   _____

3. Scott was filled with sorrow at the condition in which he found many of the churches. Explain his reaction.

   _____
   _____
   _____

4. What did Scott find to be the central truth of the Christian faith? (He called it the "golden oracle.")

   _____
   _____
   _____

5. How were Walter Scott and Alexander Campbell different in their natures and ministries?

   _____
   _____
   _____

B. Walter Scott coupled his oratory abilities with the pure truth of the Word and discovered that people responded zealously to his Gospel invitations.

1. What was the invitation that Scott offered on his first evangelistic tour for the Mahoning Association?

   _____
   _____

2. What was the one fact that had eluded Scott up to the time of his discussion with Jacob Osborne?

   _____
   _____
   _____

3. Explain the "Five-finger Exercise" used by Scott.

   _____
   _____
   _____
   _____
   _____
   _____
   _____

4. What was Thomas Campbell's evaluation of Walter Scott's preaching and invitation?

   _____
   _____
   _____

5. Scott also published a journal. What was its title?

C. While not honored through physical monuments after his death, Scott has been honored through a living monument.

1. What is that living monument?

   _____

   _____

   _____

2. How did Alexander Campbell respond to the news of Walter Scott's death?

   _____

   _____

   _____

Your Turn for Questions

What questions do you have about what you have studied in chapter nine?

_____

_____

_____

_____

What About You?

1. If you had been asked to write an epitaph for the tombstone of Walter Scott, what would you have written?

   _____

   _____

   _____

2. God wants us to be His instruments through which He will speak His gospel of Jesus Christ. With whom do you need to share that message?

   _____

   _____

3. What effect are these brief biographical sketches having on you?

   _____

   _____

   _____

   _____

THE WAY TO BECOME A CHRISTIAN IS TO BELIEVE IN CHRIST, REPENT OF SINS, BE BAPTIZED, AND RECEIVE THE FORGIVENESS OF SINS AND THE GIFT OF THE HOLY SPIRIT

Chapter Ten

SIN

The great chasm between man and God.

Key Verse

"Wherefore, as by one man sin entered into the world, and death by sin; and so death passed upon all men, for that all have sinned."

Romans 5:12

Recapitulation:
The way to become a Christian is to believe in Christ, repent of sins, be baptized, and receive the forgiveness of sins and the gift of the Holy Spirit.

What to Expect

A clear presentation of the fact of and the results of sin.

A motivation to resolve, through God's grace, to be restored to fellowship with Him.

Dealing With the Issues

A. Perhaps a part of the problem with evangelistic appeals today is that they are too complicated. Scott clarified the truth of the gospel in a simple fashion.

1. What is the first realization to which a non-Christian must come?

   _____
   _____
   _____

2. Give and explain the most often used Greek word for *sin*.

   _____
   _____
   _____

3. For what purpose does the Scripture tell us man was created by God?

   _____
   _____
   _____

4. List and explain in your own words the three classifications of sin.

   a. _____
   _____
   _____

   b. _____
   _____
   _____

   c. _____
   _____
   _____

5. Relate these Scriptures to the above categories. (Circle a, b, or c.)

   a. 1 John 3:4   a b c

   b. James 1:14, 15 a b c

   c. James 4:17   a b c

   d. 1 John 5:10   a b c

B. Both the Old and New Testaments have much to say concerning the subject of sin. Give your understanding of the following passages.

1. Romans 3:23 _____
   _____
   _____

2. Isaiah 53:6 _____
   _____
   _____

3. 1 John 1:10 _____
   _____
   _____

4. Genesis 2:9 _____
   _____
   _____

5. Genesis 2:18 _____
   _____
   _____

C. Satan entered the scene of mankind as early as the opening chapters of the book of Genesis. He still plagues mankind after centuries of exacting evil upon God's world.

1. How does the Bible refer to Satan?

   _____
   _____

2. What has been Satan's greatest delusion to mankind?

3. Describe the three deaths that the Bible says will occur as a result of sin.

   a.

   b.

   c.

4. In light of the presence of sin, what can we not expect, and for what can we hope?

Your Turn for Questions

What questions do you have about what you have studied in chapter ten?

What About You?

1. Recall your first realization of sin in your life. What were your thoughts and impressions?

2. Sin is a terrible evil in this world, but God is greater than our sin and has provided a way of escape from the awful punishment of sin. Take a moment to express your thankfulness to Him in a prayer that you can write out here.

THE WAGES OF SIN IS DEATH, AND ALL HAVE SINNED

Chapter Eleven

GRACE

The bridge to fellowship with God.

Key Verses

"For by grace are ye saved through faith; and that not of yourselves: it is the gift of God: not of works, lest any man should boast."

Ephesians 2:8, 9

Recapitulation: The wages of sin is death.

What to Expect

A deeper understanding of the background and significance of the term and concept of *grace*.

A fuller comprehension of the implications of grace.

Dealing With the Issues

A. The wages of sin is death! That fact alone leaves man in a terrible condition: alienated from the Person and presence of Almighty God. We praise Him, however, that through His matchless grace, we can have a certainty of salvation on which to rest our hope.

1. How does the Bible describe Hell?

2. Why is it futile for man to compare himself to other men with regard to goodness?

3. Record a few of your impressions as you consider Paul's words in Romans 5:8.

4. Give the two-fold prophecy of Genesis 3:15.

   a.

   b.

5. What do the following prophetic passages say about the subject of man's sin and/or God's grace.

   a. Revelation 13:8

   b. Isaiah 53:5, 6

   c. Matthew 1:21

6. Why was it necessary for Jesus to be without sin in His life?

7. What three facts does the cross reveal to us?

   a.

   b.

   c.

B. The term *grace* is filled with beauty and meaning, especially for Christians. We have tasted first-hand of the transforming power of God's grace through the Person and work of Jesus Christ in His sacrificial atonement for our sin.

1. Give some of the background meaning of the word *grace*.

   _____

   _____

   _____

2. Define, in your own words, the following terms as they relate to the subject of grace.

   a. Atonement_____

   _____

   _____

   b. Justification_____

   _____

   _____

   c. Redemption_____

   _____

   _____

   d. Reconciliation_____

   _____

   _____

Your Turn for Questions

What questions do you have about what you have studied in chapter eleven?

_____

_____

_____

_____

What About You?

1. Have you truly come to grips with your own sense of lostness apart from the grace of God? Ponder, for a moment, the sinfulness of your own life and renew your appreciation for His gift of salvation to you. Express your appreciation below.

   _____

   _____

   _____

2. Take some time to go through your Bible concordance looking up the word *grace*. Begin checking the references and make a list of the various meanings and applications of this uniquely beautiful concept.

   _____

   _____

   _____

3. Locate the words to the song "Amazing Grace," and read them aloud as if to pray them audibly to God in thanksgiving.

CHRIST PAID THE PENALTY FOR OUR SINS IN HIS DEATH ON THE CROSS

Chapter Twelve
FAITH

Key Verses

"But without faith it is impossible to please him: for he that cometh to God must believe that he is, and that he is a rewarder of them that diligently seek him."

Hebrews 11:6

Recapitulation: The wages of sin is death, but by grace you are saved.

What to Expect

A knowledge of how the word *faith* is used in the Scriptures.

An appreciation for how faith was lived out in the lives of Old Testament servants.

Dealing With the Issues

A. God has accomplished the work of salvation. It is only up to us to receive His gift by means of our faith. Throughout the Old and New Testaments, we see faith demonstrated in the lives of those who would be followers of God. The Lord's demands are no less for us. He expects us to respond to Him with faith.

1. In what three ways does the Bible use the term *faith*?

    a. _____

    b. _____

    c. _____

2. What is the meaning of Hebrews 11:1?

3. Describe how Noah exhibited faith in his life.

4. Describe how Abraham exhibited faith in his life.

5. How could Abraham go through with the Lord's command to execute his own son?

6. Do a little more thinking and studying over these Old Testament faith examples and come up with three principles of faith we learn from them.

    a. _____

    b. _____

    c. _____

B. Although we are exhorted to walk by faith and not by sight, we often fail to trust completely in our Lord. It is possible to stray so far from His desired will for us that we walk through life almost completely by sight, rather than by our trust in God. How unfortunate for us when He has made His intentions to provide for us so very clear!

1. Comment briefly on the following passages as they speak to the subject of faith.

   a. Mark 16:16 _____

   _____

   _____

   b. Acts 16:30, 31 _____

   _____

   _____

2. Paul said in Romans 10:17, "So then faith cometh by hearing, and hearing by the word of God." What is your understanding of this verse?

   _____

   _____

   _____

   _____

3. "Faith is essential to salvation." Do you agree with this statement? Why or why not?

   _____

   _____

   _____

4. What is the relationship of faith to the Word of God?

   _____

   _____

Your Turn for Questions

What questions do you have about what you have studied in chapter twelve?

_____

_____

_____

_____

_____

What About You?

1. Make a list of the important elements of "the faith." How well do you understand these concepts? Ask your teacher, preacher, or an elder for some help in knowing more about these matters.

   _____

   _____

   _____

2. Think back over your life in Christ. Evaluate your faith action and decide upon some ways to improve your faith-responsiveness to God's will.

   _____

   _____

   _____

   _____

   _____

FAITH MEANS TO BELIEVE GOD'S WORD AND TRUST HIS PROMISES

Chapter Thirteen

REPENTANCE

"We must turn from sin to walk in righteousness."

Key Verses

"And the times of this ignorance God winked at; but now commandeth all men every where to repent: because he hath appointed a day, in the which he will judge the world in righteousness by that man whom he hath ordained; whereof he hath given assurance unto all men, in that he hath raised him from the dead."

Acts 17:30, 31

Recapitulation: Faith means to believe God's Word and trust His promises.

What to Expect

A clear understanding of the concept of repentance.

A reminder of how repentance has been woven through the Scriptures.

Dealing With the Issues

A. God has always required man to respond to Him with a change of mind and heart. "Return to me!" cried the prophets as they spoke for the Lord. God's love is unconditional; however, His grace is conditioned on our faithful response. There is the imperative "if."

1. How do you define a Gospel sermon?

2. In what way did Peter convict his audience on the day of Pentecost?

3. What evidence is there that Peter made believers of his listeners?

4. Explain in your own words the message of Acts 17:30, 31.

5. How did each of the following preach a message of repentance?

   a. Jonah

   b. Ezekiel

   c. John the Baptist

   d. Jesus

B. The more we understand the concept of repentance, the more we can follow our Lord in a spirit of repentance.

1. Give the background meaning of the word *repentance*.

2. What did McGarvey have to say about repentance?

3. Explain the relationship of Godly sorrow and repentance.

4. How is one brought to the Godly sorrow that causes repentance?

5. How is the restoration concept of repentance distinct from Calvinistic teaching?

6. Our text gives three ways in which the Word of God leads one to repentance. List them below and offer your own comments about each.

   a.

   b.

   c.

7. Do you agree with McGarvey's opinion that the greatest difficulty in bringing one into Christ lies in the stubborn will? Support your answer with Scripture and perhaps personal experience.

Your Turn for Questions

What questions do you have about what you have studied in chapter thirteen?

What About You?

1. What is the most compelling message of God's word that has been the instrument of your own repentant heart?

2. Whom do you know that is caught in stubbornness? Write their names below and pray for them individually.

_____

_____

_____

3. Verbalize your personal commitment to Jesus Christ once again and reconfirm your willingness to serve Him.

_____

_____

_____

EXCEPT YOU REPENT AND BECOME A CHRISTIAN, YOU WILL PERISH

Chapter Fourteen

THE GOOD CONFESSION

Key Verses

"When Jesus came into the coasts of Caesarea Philippi, he asked his disciples, saying, Whom do men say that I, the Son of man, am? ... And Simon Peter answered and said, Thou art the Christ, the Son of the living God."
Matthew 16:13, 16

Recapitulation: Repentance is the willful decision to become a Christian.

What to Expect

A clearer perception of the roles Jesus has fulfilled as the Christ.

An appreciation of the grave nature of confession in the witness of the Christian.

Dealing With the Issues

A. A confession is a profession of one's change in identity. The word means "to say the same thing"; that is, to agree with what the Lord has said. When a person accepts Christ as Savior and Lord, he is agreeing with all the Lord has said.

1. What did Walter Scott call the confession found in Matthew 16:16?

   _____

   _____

2. Interpret Walter Scott's words: "The Holy Book contains one truth which is the sun to which all other Christian truths are planets in a spiritual solar system."

   _____

   _____

   _____

   _____

3. Our text states that the background of the good confession is found in John 9. What is the background of the confession?

   _____

   _____

   _____

4. How significant was Peter's response to Jesus in Matthew 16 as contrasted to that of the others? Explain.

   _____

   _____

   _____

   _____

B. The truth of Peter's confession comprises the foundation of Christianity. Jesus is the Christ! Our lives must reflect our testimony to that glorious truth.

1. What is the meaning in the title *Christ*?

   _____

   _____

   _____

2. What does the name *Jesus* mean?

   _____

   _____

3. How do the following passages reinforce the fact of Christ's kingship?

   a. Matthew 27:11 _____

   _____

   _____

   b. Matthew 2:2 _____

   _____

   _____

   c. Luke 1:32, 33 _____

   _____

   _____

   d. John 1:49 _____

   _____

   _____

   e. Revelation 17:14; 19:16 _____

   _____

   _____

4. In what ways has Jesus Christ served as high priest?

   _____
   _____
   _____
   _____
   _____

5. How did Jesus Christ fulfill the role of prophet?

   _____
   _____
   _____
   _____
   _____

6. What three truths does one accept when confessing Jesus as the Christ?

   a. _____
   _____

   b. _____
   _____

   c. _____
   _____

7. List some Scripture passages that testify that Jesus was God in the flesh.

   _____
   _____
   _____

Your Turn for Questions

What questions do you have about what you have read in chapter fourteen?

_____
_____
_____
_____
_____
_____

What About You?

1. Say aloud the confession of your faith in Jesus as the Christ. What does that confession mean to you personally?

   _____
   _____
   _____

2. How is it possible for us to contradict our confession with our behavior and speech?

   _____
   _____
   _____

3. The real value of our confession of faith is seen when it is made before the non-Christian world. Determine before God that you will be a consistent witness for Jesus Christ in your every walk of life. Write a statement of your commitment below.

   _____
   _____
   _____

**THE GOOD CONFESSION EXPRESSES
ONE'S DESIRE TO BECOME A CHRISTIAN**

Chapter Fifteen

THE MEANING OF CHRISTIAN BAPTISM

In baptism, one dies to the old life and is born again to the new life.

Key Verse

"Then Peter said unto them, Repent and be baptized every one of you in the name of Jesus Christ for the remission of sins, and ye shall receive the gift of the Holy Ghost."

Acts 2:38

Recapitulation: The Good Confession expresses one's desire to become a Christian.

What to Expect

A synopsis of Jesus' teaching about baptism.

The New Testament presentation of baptism as it pertains to salvation.

Dealing With the Issues

A. Christian baptism has been a source of controversy and, unfortunately, even division. Let us examine the Scriptures to determine the truth about this act of faith.

1. Why did Walter Scott refer to baptism as the "missing link" in his *Gospel Restored?*

   _____
   _____
   _____
   _____

2. Why cannot the believer take baptism lightly?

   _____
   _____
   _____
   _____

3. What does the account of the events on the Day of Pentecost tell us concerning baptism?

   _____
   _____
   _____
   _____
   _____

4. How are we to understand Peter's words in 1 Peter 3:21?

   _____
   _____
   _____
   _____

B. A common phrase used by contemporary Christians is "born again." Baptism presents a perfect picture of the rebirthing that takes place when the believer has died to sin.

1. What point does B. W. Johnson make regarding the account of Jesus with Nicodemus?

   _____
   _____
   _____
   _____

2. Give your own summation of the conversion of Saul of Tarsus.

   _____
   _____
   _____
   _____
   _____
   _____

3. Comment briefly on the following passages as they relate to our discussion of baptism.

   a. Romans 6:3_____
   _____
   _____

   b. Romans 5:9_____
   _____
   _____

   c. Revelation 1:5_____
   _____
   _____

   d. Ephesians 1:7_____
   _____
   _____

4. What is the purpose of baptism in the plan of salvation?

5. What gift is ours as a result of baptism?

6. Why is Christian baptism not merely "water regeneration"?

7. List and give your appraisal of the alternatives to the view of Christian baptism presented in the text.

   a.

   b.

Your Turn for Questions

What questions do you have about what you have studied in chapter fifteen?

What About You?

1. Recall your own baptism and reflect on its meaning.

2. Why do you suppose baptism has been so controversial through the years?

3. Plan to make a personal study of baptism from the New Testament, making use of your concordance, Bible commentaries, and other reference tools.

4. Fill in the following chart. Put an "X" where a step in the plan of salvation is explicitly mentioned, and an "O" where it is just implied.

CONVERSIONS IN ACTS					
	Hearing the Gospel	Faith	Repent	Confess	Baptism
3000 on Pentecost Acts 2					
Ethiopian Treasurer Acts 8					
Cornelius Acts 10					
Saul of Tarsus Acts 9, 22, 26					
Philippian Jailer Acts 16					
Lydia Acts 16					

**CHRISTIAN BAPTISM IS THE CLIMAX
OF ONE'S ACCEPTANCE OF CHRIST IN FAITH**

Chapter Sixteen

THE MODE AND SUBJECTS OF CHRISTIAN BAPTISM

In the likeness of Christ's death, burial, and resurrection.

Key Verses

"Know ye not, that so many of us as were baptized into Jesus Christ were baptized into his death? Therefore we are buried with him by baptism into death: that like as Christ was raised up from the dead by the glory of the Father, even so we also should walk in newness of life."

Romans 6:3, 4

Recapitulation:
Christian baptism is the climax of one's acceptance of Christ in faith.

What to Expect

A background of the English word *baptism*.

An explanation of how variant forms of baptism have come to be accepted in religion.

Dealing With the Issues

A. We have seen how the plan of salvation relates to one's mind, will, identity, and, finally, one's state or relationship with God. The question of the mode and subjects for baptism must also be addressed for us to complete our understanding of the subject.

1. At what point in his life did Alexander Campbell face up to the question of the mode of Christian baptism?

   _____

   _____

   _____

2. What does the word *immersion* mean?

   _____

   _____

3. Explain the symbolism in Jewish proselyte baptism.

   _____

   _____

   _____

   _____

4. Share some of the New Testament evidence that baptism is immersion.

   _____

   _____

   _____

   _____

5. What did the apostle Paul write to the Christians at Rome that helps us answer the question, "What is Christian baptism?"

   _____

   _____

   _____

   _____

   _____

B. Christian baptism is not only an act, but a re-enactment, in a real sense. Paul was most explicit about this in his writing to the Roman Christians.

1. What two dramatic truths does Paul say are portrayed in baptism?

   a. _____

   _____

   _____

   b. _____

   _____

   _____

2. How is a transliteration different from a translation?

   _____

   _____

   _____

3. In what other ways is the word *baptism* or a form of it used in the New Testament?

   _____

   _____

   _____

   _____

4. What did the following men say about baptism?

   a. Martin Luther _____
   _____
   _____

   b. John Calvin _____
   _____
   _____

   c. P. H. Welshimer _____
   _____
   _____

5. What prerequisites to Christian baptism make it inappropriate for infants?
   _____
   _____
   _____
   _____

6. Why did infant baptism appear in the church?
   _____
   _____
   _____

Your Turn for Questions

What questions do you have about what you have studied in chapter sixteen?
_____
_____
_____
_____
_____

What About You?

1. Giving up traditions is difficult for any of us. What are some of the beliefs you have abandoned since beginning your walk with the Lord?
   _____
   _____
   _____
   _____

2. Straying from God's Word is a temptation to us all. What are you doing to avoid such a pitfall?
   _____
   _____
   _____
   _____

**CHRISTIAN BAPTISM IS THE IMMERSION
OF A REPENTANT BELIEVER FOR THE REMISSION OF SINS
THAT HE MIGHT RECEIVE THE GIFT OF THE HOLY SPIRIT**

Chapter Seventeen

THE HOLY SPIRIT

"What! know ye not that your body is the temple of the Holy Ghost, which is in you, which ye have of God?"
—1 Corinthians 6:19

Key Verses

"But ye are not in the flesh, but in the Spirit, if so be that the Spirit of God dwell in you. Now if any man have not the Spirit of Christ, he is none of his."

Romans 8:9

"And be not drunk with wine, wherein is excess; but be filled with the Spirit."

Ephesians 5:18

Recapitulation: Christian baptism is the immersion of a repentant believer for the remission of sins that he might receive the gift of the Holy Spirit.

What to Expect

An introduction to the role of the Holy Spirit in the life of the Christian.

A caution about stifling the work of the Holy Spirit in the life of the Christian.

Dealing With the Issues

A. As our text states, "The Holy Spirit, through the apostles, shaped the New Testament church" (page 133). Given such a profound truth, it behooves us to examine the role of the Holy Spirit in the life of the Christian.

1. What is the doctrine of "election," which the early restoration leaders rejected?

   _____
   _____
   _____

2. How have you been able to understand the concept of the Trinity?

   _____
   _____
   _____
   _____

3. Cite an example from the Old Testament that indicates the presence of the three Persons in the Godhead.

   _____
   _____
   _____

4. Why would J. W. McGarvey have wanted to label the book of Acts the "Acts of the Holy Spirit"?

   _____
   _____
   _____

5. What is the "gift of the Holy Spirit"?

   _____
   _____
   _____
   _____

6. How does the "gift of the Holy Spirit" differ from "gifts of the Holy Spirit"?

   _____
   _____
   _____
   _____
   _____

B. With God's Holy Spirit within us, we have become the temples. What a beautiful and awesome privilege is ours to be sanctuaries for the Spirit of God.

1. Distinguish the "gift" of the Holy Spirit from the "filling" of the Holy Spirit.

   _____
   _____
   _____

2. What is the best way to "test the spirits"?

   _____
   _____
   _____

3. How does Ephesians 4:32 shed light on how one might "grieve the Holy Spirit"?

   _____
   _____
   _____
   _____

4. What happens to the person who receives the gift of the Holy Spirit, who is filled with the Spirit, and who walks in the Spirit?

   _____
   _____
   _____
   _____

5. Give your own brief understanding of each of the following aspects of the fruit of the Spirit. (See Galatians 5:22, 23.)

   a. Love _____

   b. Joy _____

   c. Peace _____

   d. Long-suffering _____

   e. Gentleness _____

   f. Goodness _____

   g. Faith _____

   h. Meekness _____

   i. Temperance _____

Your Turn for Questions

What questions do you have about what you have studied in chapter seventeen?

What About You?

1. In what ways have you depersonalized the Holy Spirit?

   _____

   _____

   _____

   _____

2. Are you walking in the Holy Spirit? How do you know?

   _____

   _____

   _____

3. Make some specific applications this week to develop a greater demonstration of the fruit of the Spirit in your life.

> **THE GIFT OF THE HOLY SPIRIT
> IS THE INDWELLING PRESENCE OF CHRIST
> IN THE CHRISTIANS'S LIFE
> THAT ENABLES HIM TO BECOME MORE LIKE CHRIST**

Chapter Eighteen

MEMBERSHIP AND MINISTRY

Key Verses

"Having then gifts differing according to the grace that is given to us, whether prophecy, let us prophesy according to the proportion of faith; or ministry, let us wait on our ministering; or he that teacheth, on teaching; or he that exhorteth, on exhortation: he that giveth, let him do it with simplicity; he that ruleth, with diligence; he that sheweth mercy, with cheerfulness."

Romans 12:6-8

Recapitulation: The gift of the Holy Spirit is the indwelling presence of Christ in the Christian's life that enables him to become more like Him.

What to Expect

To be challenged with the admonition to discover and develop your spiritual gift.

An appeal for mutual ministry within the body of Christ.

Dealing With the Issues

A. It has been said that "blood is thicker than water," an obvious reference to loyalties to family. The truth of that phrase is nowhere more relevant than its application to the household of God, united through the blood of our elder brother, Jesus Christ.

1. How do the following passages reflect Christ's love for the church?

   a. Ephesians 5:25 _____

   b. Acts 20:28 _____

2. Respond to the statement in our text: "Church membership is not optional for the Christian."

3. Why is it important for a Christian to identify with a local congregation?

4. Why is the clergy-laity concept not valid for the church of Jesus Christ?

5. Make some notes about the following passages referring to the gifts of the Spirit.

   a. 1 Corinthians 12:4-12 _____

   b. 1 Corinthians 12:27-31 _____

   c. Romans 12:4-8 _____

   d. Ephesians 4:11-16 _____

   e. 1 Peter 4:10, 11 _____

B. Our Lord has blessed each of His children with gifts to be used in service for the sake of His Kingdom. The sincere Christian will make every effort to identify, develop, and utilize his gift for the glory of Christ.

1. What are the four groups in which miracles appear in Scripture?

    a. _____

    b. _____

    c. _____

    d. _____

2. What principles can you glean from 1 Corinthians 12:14-20?

3. Is there Scriptural precedent for a person receiving wages for service in the church? Explain and cite Scripture references.

4. What examples of ministry do we learn from the Jerusalem church?

Your Turn for Questions

What questions do you have about what you have studied in chapter eighteen?

What About You?

1. How are you presently ministering in your local congregation?

2. Have you identified your spiritual gift? If not, talk with a spiritual advisor about how to discover your particular gift. Record some ideas below.

   _____

   _____

   _____

   _____

   _____

3. Consider some of the ways you may have subtly offended others in the church who have different gifts from yours. Make restitution for your offense and be reconciled to your brother or sister.

   Who may have been offended?_____

   _____

   How to be reconciled:_____

   _____

   _____

**EVERY CHRISTIAN RECEIVES HIS GIFT
TO BE USED TO BLESS THE LIVES OF OTHERS
AND TO MAKE THE CHURCH STRONG**

Chapter Nineteen

EVANGELISM AND DISCIPLESHIP

"John Q. Evangelist" joins "John Q. Discipler."

Key Verses

"And he gave some, apostles; and some, prophets; and some, evangelists; and some, pastors and teachers; for the perfecting of the saints, for the work of the ministry, for the edifying of the body of Christ: till we all come in the unity of the faith, and of the knowledge of the Son of God, unto a perfect man, unto the measure of the stature of the fulness of Christ...."

Ephesians 4:11-13

Recapitulation: Every Christian receives his gift to be used to bless the lives of others and to make the church strong.

What to Expect

An overview of the subject of evangelism from the New Testament.

Practical advice about growing in Jesus Christ toward spiritual maturity.

Dealing With the Issues

A. God has never said that the Christian life would be a life of ease. In fact, just the opposite is true. As we read in the Scriptures, we see that we are involved in spiritual warfare.

1. Paul said that we are not wrestling against flesh and blood, but against what?

   _____

   _____

   _____

2. What are the two major areas of spiritual service?

   a. _____

   b. _____

3. What is the definition of *evangelism*?

   _____

   _____

   _____

   _____

4. In what two ways is the word *evangelist* used in the New Testament?

   a. _____

   _____

   b. _____

   _____

5. How did God bring good out of the persecution work of Paul?

   _____

   _____

   _____

   _____

6. Why is it impossible for a Christian to fail as an evangelist if he presents the gospel in a loving, winsome way?

   _____

   _____

   _____

   _____

B. Christians must keep in mind their obligation to spread the Gospel of Jesus Christ, realizing that the outcome is not in our hands. People will respond to the message according to their own will.

1. Recount the parable of the Sower, indicating who is represented in each case.

   _____

   _____

   _____

   _____

   _____

   _____

   _____

   _____

   _____

   _____

   _____

   _____

   _____

   _____

   _____

   _____

   _____

   _____

2. What is meant by the following terms?

   a. Discipleship _____
   _____
   _____
   _____

   b. Edification _____
   _____
   _____
   _____

   c. Perfection _____
   _____
   _____
   _____

3. In what ways is the Word an instrument of our growth in Christ?
   _____
   _____
   _____
   _____
   _____

4. In what ways is prayer an instrument of our growth in Christ?
   _____
   _____
   _____
   _____
   _____
   _____

5. In what ways is fellowship an instrument of our growth in Christ?
   _____
   _____
   _____
   _____
   _____
   _____
   _____

6. In what ways is exercise an instrument of our growth in Christ?
   _____
   _____
   _____
   _____
   _____
   _____
   _____

Your Turn for Questions

What questions do you have about what you have studied in chapter nineteen?

_____
_____
_____
_____
_____
_____
_____
_____

What About You?

1. Whom have you influenced with the message of the Gospel of Jesus Christ? Recall the names of individuals in whose lives you have played the role of evangelist.

   _____

   _____

   _____

2. What is your local congregation doing to support the work of missions? Do some research and questioning to find out if you don't know.

   _____

   _____

   _____

3. Visit your local Christian bookstore and purchase at least one good resource on the subject of discipleship. Study up!

PERSONS MUST BE BROUGHT INTO CHRIST AND HELPED TO GROW STRONG IN HIM

Chapter Twenty

CHRISTIAN WORSHIP

Key Verses

"And let us consider one another to provoke unto love and to good works: not forsaking the assembling of ourselves together, as the manner of some is; but exhorting one another: and so much the more, as ye see the day approaching."

Hebrews 10:24, 25

Recapitulation: Persons must be brought into Christ and helped to grow strong in Him.

What to Expect

An increased understanding of the term *worship*.

A review of the early church practices in corporate worship.

Dealing with the Issues

A. Worship is more of a response to God than anything initiated on our part. In light of who God is, we worship Him.

1. Do you agree with the statement in our text (page 161): "One cannot even be religious unless he worships"? Explain.

2. Give some of the etymological background of the word *worship*.

3. What are some of the results of corporate Christian worship?

4. Acts 2:42 reveals four key elements of early Christian worship. Identify each one and explain whether you see it in practice in today's church.

   a.

   b.

   c.

   d.

5. Paul exhorts that when partaking of the Lord's Supper, our thoughts should go in three directions. Name them and give the Scripture reference for each.

   a.

   b.

   c.

B. It can be very easy for traditions to push out Biblical mandates and precedents. Caution must always be taken to protect the divine elements from exclusion in our corporate worship.

1. Two additional practices are cited in our text that may have been integral parts of early Christian services. What are they?

    a. _____

    b. _____

2. Why did God choose Sunday as the day for corporate worship?

    _____
    _____
    _____

Your Turn for Questions

What questions do you have about what you have studied in chapter twenty?

_____
_____
_____
_____
_____

What About You?

1. Read through a Psalm each day this week and meditate on the greatness of God's glory. Worship Him through your quiet time. List the Psalms you use.

    _____
    _____
    _____
    _____
    _____
    _____
    _____

2. Have you begun to take the Lord's Supper for granted. Offer a written prayer praising and thanking God for His sacrificial offering to you. Give Him your sacrificial offering of praise.

    _____
    _____
    _____
    _____
    _____
    _____

**CHRISTIANS GATHER ON THE LORD'S DAY
WITH THE LORD'S PEOPLE AROUND THE LORD'S TABLE
TO PARTAKE OF THE LORD'S SUPPER
IN THE WORSHIP OF THE LORD**

Chapter Twenty-One

CHURCH GOVERNMENT

Each part working together makes a whole.

Key Verses

"Obey them that have the rule over you, and submit yourselves: for they watch for your souls, as they that must give an account, that they may do it with joy, and not with grief: for that is unprofitable for you."
Hebrews 13:17

Recapitulation: Christians gather on the Lord's Day with the Lord's people around the Lord's table to partake of the Lord's Supper in the worship of the Lord.

What to Expect

A glimpse at variant church organizational structures in religion.

An impression of the New Testament offices and their relativity to the present church practice.

Dealing With the Issues

A. Leaders and managers have developed numerous procedures and policies for governments and organizations, which have often proved themselves effective. The church, however, must do more than find a practice that is effective. It must find and incorporate the practice that is Biblical.

1. Summarize briefly the ecclesiastical hierarchy of the Roman Catholic Church.

   _____
   _____
   _____
   _____

2. Give the basic governmental structure of the Greek Orthodox Church.

   _____
   _____
   _____
   _____

3. What specific recommendations did Barton Stone make regarding church organization in the *Last Will and Testament of the Springfield Presbytery?*

   _____
   _____
   _____

4. What was Alexander Campbell's advice about church structure?

   _____
   _____
   _____

5. How do you understand the concept of local autonomy?

   _____
   _____
   _____
   _____
   _____

B. The early church did not have the struggle with organizational confusion that often plagues the present-day church, primarily because of the supervision of the apostles. There was organization, however, and different ministries or offices in the early church.

1. What were some of the credentials of the apostles that made them such capable leaders of the Lord's church?

   _____
   _____
   _____
   _____

2. List the three divinely appointed places of service in the church.

   a. _____
   b. _____
   c. _____

3. What are the three Greek terms used to denote the office of elder, and what is the significance of each?

   a. _____
   _____
   b. _____
   _____
   c. _____
   _____

4. Use the following Scriptures to list some qualities of the men who should serve as elders.

   a. Titus 1:5-9 _____

   b. 1 Timothy 3:1-7 _____

5. What is the meaning of the Greek word *diakonos*?

6. Using 1 Timothy 3:8-13 as a guide, what are the qualities for the office of deacon?

7. What is meant by the phrase "elder rule"?

8. Give the four principles of leadership suggested in the text for the church to receive God's blessing.

   a. _____

   b. _____

   c. _____

   d. _____

Your Turn for Questions

What questions do you have about what you have studied in chapter twenty-one?

What About You?

1. A few of the various types of church organizations are mentioned in our text. What other variations have you noticed in other churches?

   _____

   _____

   _____

   _____

2. How can we improve our practice of church polity and become more of a New Testament church?

   _____

   _____

   _____

   _____

CHRIST'S CHURCH NEEDS DEDICATED LEADERS WHO WILL SERVE AND LOVE HIS PEOPLE

Chapter Twenty-Two

CHRISTIAN STEWARDSHIP

"Everything I have and everything I am are God's."

Key Verse

"The earth is the Lord's, and the fulness thereof; the world, and they that dwell therein."

Psalm 24:1

Recapitulation: Christ's church needs dedicated leaders who will serve and love His people.

What to Expect

A reminder of God's standards of stewardship.

Guidelines about your giving to the Lord's work.

Dealing With the Issues

A. God has always been concerned about how a man handles his material possessions. His requirement has been the first-fruits of our harvest. He is equally concerned with how we invest the balance of our wealth as He is with our tithes and offerings.

1. What can be learned from the parable of the talents?

   _____
   _____
   _____
   _____

2. What is the point of Job's words in Job 1:21?

   _____
   _____
   _____

3. Comment on the following passages as they address the subject of stewardship.

   a. 1 Corinthians 6:19, 20 _____
   _____
   _____
   _____

   b. Romans 12:1 _____
   _____
   _____
   _____

   c. 1 Corinthians 4:2 _____
   _____
   _____
   _____

B. Frances Schaeffer wrote a book entitled, *No Little People*, in which he promoted the fact that in God's kingdom, each person is of inestimable value.

1. How do Moses, Paul, and John Wesley demonstrate this truth in and through their ministries?

   _____
   _____
   _____
   _____
   _____

2. Give a little of the history of the tithe.

   _____
   _____
   _____

3. Malachi had a message about God's blessings for those who trust in Him and demonstrate that trust through faithful stewardship. What is that message from Malachi 3:10?

   _____
   _____
   _____

4. Our text gives four guidelines for the Christian concerning his giving. List them below and comment on each.

   a. _____
   _____

   b. _____
   _____

   c. _____
   _____

   d. _____
   _____

5. What does Paul teach us about stewardship in 2 Corinthians 9:6?

_____

_____

_____

6. What is the goal of the good steward?

_____

_____

_____

Your Turn for Questions

What questions do you have about what you have studied in chapter twenty-two?

_____

_____

_____

_____

What About You?

1. Do some private introspection about your spending habits. Take the past year, or month, or even just the past week. How did you spend your paycheck? How much went to personal gratification? How much went to the Lord's work?

_____

_____

_____

_____

2. How can you adjust your budget to give more to the Lord?

_____

_____

_____

3. Consider how you have been spending your time lately. Is God receiving the first-fruits of your time each day? Start your day with God by reading a portion of His Word and talking with Him in prayer. Begin tomorrow morning. The formula is simple: "Refuse to be fed physically until you have been fed spiritually!"

**ALL THE CHRISTIAN HAS OR IS
BELONGS TO GOD BY RIGHT OF CREATION
AND SHOULD BE USED TO BRING A PROFIT TO HIS HOUSEHOLD**

Chapter Twenty-Three

THE ACAPPELLA CHURCHES OF CHRIST

Key Verses

"And be not drunk with wine, wherein is excess; but be filled with the Spirit; speaking to yourselves in psalms and hymns and spiritual songs, singing and making melody in your heart to the Lord; giving thanks always for all things unto God the Father in the name of our Lord Jesus Christ; submitting yourselves one to another in the fear of God."

Ephesians 5:18-21

Recapitulation: All the Christian has or is belongs to God by right of creation and should be used to bring a profit to His household.

What to Expect

A brief history of the non-instrumental Churches of Christ.

A challenge to fulfill the ideal of being Christians only instead of the only Christians.

Dealing With the Issues

A. It is always sad to see division within the church. Such is especially true when the division seems to be unwarranted. We can be encouraged at recent attempts to reunite with our noninstrumental brothers in Christ.

1. Share some of the facts about the Churches of Christ that you learned from the text.

2. Identify and characterize the six groups found within the Churches of Christ.

   a. _____

   b. _____

   c. _____

   d. _____

   e. _____

   f. _____

3. What marked the official separation of the Churches of Christ from the rest of the restoration movement?

4. Explain the contents and implications of *The Sand Creek Declaration*.

B. Historical and sociological factors usually play an important role in church factions. The division of which we speak was no exception.

1. What were some of the cultural issues around this matter of the instrument?

2. How is it that Ephesians 5:19 is the crucial verse for the acappella argument?

3. What is meant by an argument from silence?

4. Explain the law of exclusion.

5. How did R. M. Bell reason that instruments were used in the New Testament church?

6. In what ways have we, as a movement, contradicted the stance of being "Christians only and not the only Christians?"

7. What were the four benefits gained as a result of the meetings between noninstrumental church leaders and those of the instrumental churches?

   a.

   b.

   c.

   d.

Your Turn for Questions

What questions do you have about what you have studied in chapter twenty-three?

What About You?

1. How much did you know about the noninstrumental Church of Christ prior to this lesson? Perhaps you should do some further study about other church groups.

2. In what ways are you manifesting an exclusivistic attitude about your Christianity? If you're not sure, ask those around you.

_____

_____

_____

_____

3. What can you do in your own realm of relationships to enhance understanding for Christians in other churches.

_____

_____

_____

_____

> **THE RESTORATION IDEAL LEADS BELIEVERS TO STRIVE TO BE CHRISTIANS ONLY, BUT NOT TO LOOK UPON THEMSELVES AS THE ONLY CHRISTIANS**

Chapter Twenty-Four

THE DISCIPLES OF CHRIST

Let's continue the quest of true unity for God's people based on His Word.

Key Verses

"Hold fast the form of sound words, which thou hast heard of me, in faith and love which is in Christ Jesus. That good thing which was committed unto thee keep by the Holy Ghost which dwelleth in us."
2 Timothy 1:13, 14

Recapitulation: The restoration ideal leads believers to strive to be Christians only, but not to look upon themselves as the only Christians.

What to Expect

A history of the present-day liberalism as it found its roots in evolutionism.

A background of the Disciples of Christ churches and their relationship to the restoration movement.

99

Dealing With the Issues

A. Doctrinal liberalism is a great evil that the early restorers sought to avoid at all costs. Unfortunately, ideals tend to become distorted as generations come and go. Such is the sad history of the restoration movement.

1. How did evolutionism affect the doctrinal stance within the movement?

2. What effect did World War II have upon the evolutionary thought of socialism?

3. Explain German rationalism.

4. What are some fundamental elements of the faith that modernism sought to undermine?

5. How does the modernistic approach differ from the traditional in the following areas?

   a. The Person of Jesus

   b. The Bible

   c. Miracles

   d. The Cross

   e. The Gospel

   f. The Church

B. How bitter can be the struggles and strife between men who are supposed to be brothers in Christ! Even more disheartening is the fact of vagrant abuse of the Scriptures as the absolute and true source of authority.

1. What were some of the doctrines students reported being taught at the College of the Bible soon after R. H. Crossfield took over as president?

   a. _____

   b. _____

   c. _____

   d. _____

2. What is meant by open membership?

   _____

3. What role did the North American Christian Convention play in the separation between the conservatives and the liberals?

   _____

4. Summarize the history of the conservative part of the restoration movement since the Disciples' separation.

   _____

5. Summarize the history of the Disciples Christian Churches since the separation.

   _____

Your Turn for Questions

What questions do you have about what you have studied in chapter twenty-four?

_____

What About You?

1. Have you become lazy in your appreciation of the essential doctrines of the Scripture? Examine carefully your stand on the truths of the Bible. Write a statement about your confidence in the truth, reliability, and authority of the Bible.

   _____
   _____
   _____
   _____

2. Can you see implications of evolutionism and liberalism in some of the books you have read, movies you have watched, and other forms of media?

   _____
   _____
   _____
   _____

3. Pray for the return of our movement to the unity for which our early leaders worked.

**THE FUTURE HOLDS GREAT OPPORTUNITY
FOR THOSE WHO WANT TO RESTORE THE ESSENCE
OF THE NEW TESTAMENT CHURCH TO ITS PRISTINE PURITY**

Chapter Twenty-Five

THE CHARISMATICS

We walk by faith, not by feeling.

Key Verses

"For therein is the righteousness of God revealed from faith to faith: as it is written, The just shall live by faith."

Romans 1:17

"So then faith cometh by hearing, and hearing by the word of God."

Romans 10:17

Recapitulation: The future holds great opportunity for those who want to restore the essence of the New Testament church to its pristine purity.

What to Expect

An understanding of the Pentecostal and Neo-Pentecostal movements and their intrusion into the restoration movement.

A determination to maintain Biblical revelation as the ultimate source of truth.

Dealing With the Issues

A. God's children seem not to be satisfied with the teachings of our Lord. Instead, there are always those who wish to follow Him only for the bread and the miracles.

1. What were some of the characteristics of the Pentecostals at the turn of the twentieth century?

   _____
   _____
   _____

2. How are Pentecostals and Neo-Pentecostals similar and how are they distinct?

   _____
   _____
   _____
   _____
   _____

3. What element do charismatics emphasize above all else?

   _____
   _____
   _____

4. Explain the phenomenon of *glossalalia* and how it has been perceived in church history.

   _____
   _____
   _____
   _____
   _____

B. Of utmost importance to a proper understanding of any phenomenon must be the teaching of the Scriptures. All experience and personal speculation is subject to the truth of the Bible.

1. In what three books of the New Testament can discussion of the gift of tongues be found?

   a. _____
   b. _____
   c. _____

2. Summarize Paul's treatment of the tongues issue as it appeared in the church of Corinth. How does this compare to present-day phenomena?

   _____
   _____
   _____
   _____
   _____

3. Why is it not correct to speak of tongues as a prayer language?

   _____
   _____
   _____

4. What was the purpose of the signs and miracles in the early church?

   _____
   _____
   _____
   _____

5. What are the other two emphases of the charismatics that present a threat to the ideals of the restoration movement?

   a. _____

   _____

   b. _____

   _____

Your Turn for Questions

What questions do you have about what you have studied in chapter twenty-four?

_____

_____

_____

_____

What About You?

1. Discontentment with the plain and simple truth of Scripture can lead one to search for substitutions in the form of emotionalism. Examine yourself: are your actions demonstrating that you are content with the message God has given, or are you acting more on feelings or looking for advice from other sources?

   _____

   _____

   _____

2. How many times have you been involved in a Bible study group where someone commented: "Well, regardless what the Bible says, I just feel that . . ."? Why is this a very dangerous route to take?

   _____

   _____

   _____

CHRISTIANS ARE TO BE GUIDED BY FAITH, AND NOT BY FEELINGS THAT CAN FOOL THEM.

Chapter Twenty-Six

THE FANTASTIC FUTURE FOR THE RESTORATION IDEAL

The challenge and opportunities are great!!

Key Verses

"Where there is no vision, the people perish..."
Proverbs 29:18

"That we henceforth be no more children, tossed to and fro, and carried about with every wind of doctrine, by the sleight of men, and cunning craftiness, whereby they lie in wait to deceive; but speaking the truth in love, may grow up into him in all things, which is the head, even Christ."
Ephesians 4:14, 15

Recapitulation: Christians are to be guided by faith, and not by feelings that can fool them.

What to Expect

A summary of the basic tenets of the restoration movement.

A direct and specific challenge to fulfill your role as a part of a movement attempting to discover the "restoration ideal."

Dealing With the Issues

A. The more I study and apply, the more I am reminded of the need for balance in almost every facet of life. As Christians, we must caution ourselves to balance the truth with the love of Jesus Christ.

1. What is the right creed we have to share with others in love?

    _____

    _____

2. What is the right name we have to share with others in love?

    _____

3. What is the right book we have to share with others in love?

    _____

4. What is the right church we have to share with others in love? Where can this church model be found?

    _____

    _____

5. What is the right plan of salvation we have to share with others in love?

    _____

    _____

    _____

    _____

6. What is the noblest plea we have to share with others in love?

    _____

    _____

B. In spite of the problems and separations that have occurred in the restoration movement, there is cause for great hope and encouragement with regard to our future. That hope hinges on you and your active involvement to preserve the essential values of the movement.

1. What should be the attitude of Christians who are concerned about restoring the ideal church as revealed in Scripture?

    _____

    _____

    _____

2. What attitudes must be avoided if we are to be effective in our pursuit of restoration?

    _____

    _____

    _____

    _____

3. What three practices must be prioritized in our lives and our churches if we are to fulfill the goals of the restoration movement?

    a. _____

    b. _____

    c. _____

4. What crucial steps must we take to avoid our movement's digressing into yet another denomination?

    _____

    _____

    _____

    _____

Your Turn for Questions

What questions do you have about what you have studied in chapter twenty-six?

_____
_____
_____
_____
_____
_____
_____
_____
_____
_____
_____
_____

What About You?

1. How much have you personally gained through this study of the restoration movement?

   _____
   _____
   _____
   _____

2. What changes do you need to make in your thought and in your practice to become a Christian only?

   _____
   _____
   _____
   _____

3. Take a serious moment to pray about someone with whom you might be able to share this particular book and study. Plan to purchase an extra copy of the book and workbook for that person and help him to discover the restoration ideal.

   Name_____

   When you can begin to study with this person:

   _____

A BRIGHT FUTURE APPEARS AHEAD FOR THE RESTORATION MOVEMENT

STANDARD BIBLE STUDIES

Unlocking the Scriptures for You

You'll find these new Bible studies to be just what you need to sharpen your understanding of the Scriptures covered. Each one is comprehensive, yet concise; thorough, yet uncomplicated. They are perfect for preachers, teachers, and everyone who is serious about understanding God's Word.

Matthew (40101), by LeRoy Lawson. Here's a book you can really enjoy. Lawson combines his gift for story-telling with superb exposition of the text, dealing with the Scripture in a passage-by-passage treatment.

Luke (40103), by Lewis Foster. In a unique blend of popular and scholastic styles, Foster develops his exposition in a three-level approach: overview, comprehensive passage-by-passage treatment, and summary. His original maps and charts also make this an invaluable study aid.

Hebrews (40111), by David Eubanks and Robert Shannon. Here's a delightful survey of the book of Hebrews. Eubanks has done the exposition of the text, and Shannon has added poignant application with contemporary illustrations.

Revelation (40113), by Alger Fitch. Forget the wild speculations you'll find in many studies on Revelation. Here's one that looks at the whole book from five different perspectives to uncover the message of hope that John meant to convey.

Correlated Workbooks

Use these workbooks to enhance your own study of the texts or to lead a group study. Each one combines Bible study with discussion and application questions.

Matthew (40201), by Jonathan Underwood

Luke (40203), by David Underwood

Hebrews (40211), by Michael McCann

Revelation (40213), by Timothy Heck